A BOTCHED ELECTION
Why Did the Prophets Miss It?

ALTAR BOOKS
A DIVISION OF

QUIVERFULL
PUBLISHING

A BOTCHED ELECTION
Why Did the Prophets Miss It?

© 2021 by Yvonne D. Camper

All rights reserved. No portion of this book may be reproduced, stored in a retrieval system, or transmitted in any form or by means-electronic, mechanical, photocopy, recording, scanning, or other-except for brief quotations in critical reviews or articles, without prior permission of the publisher.

Published in Fontana, California by Altar Books. A Division of Quiver Full Publishing.

Scriptures noted (NIV) are taken from the Holy Bible, New International Version®, NIV® Copyright ©1973, 1978, 1984, 2011 by Biblica, Inc.® Used by permission. All rights reserved worldwide.

Scriptures noted (NLT) are taken from the Holy Bible, New Living Translation, copyright © 1996, 2004, 2015 by Tyndale House Foundation. Used by permission of Tyndale House Publishers Inc., Carol Stream, Illinois 60188. All rights reserved.

New American Standard Bible Copyright © 1960, 1971, 1977, 1995, 2020 by The Lockman Foundation, La Habra, Calif. All rights reserved.

The Berean Bible (www.Berean.Bible) Berean Study Bible (BSB) © 2016, 2020 by Bible Hub and Berean. Bible. Used by Permission. All rights Reserved.

Scripture taken from the COMPLETE JEWISH BIBLE, copyright© 1998 by David H. Stern. Published by Jewish New Testament Publications, Inc. Int'l. www.messianicjewish.net. All rights reserved. Used by permission.

ISBN: 978-09986539-0-7

Satan hates geographical locations that have become meaningful to God and His people

Dutch Sheets, Appeal to Heaven

Use the coupon code below to download a free copy of the E-Book to access all the Links.

"Botched E-Book"

Answering the Question

    I want to start by saying I am writing this book, which was originally released as an E-book on January 22, 2021, from the place of having no interest in Politics at all. I can honestly say, I have not even voted in every election because it did not matter to me. The burden of the Lord on my life right now is by divine decree. The only thing I have vowed to do is when God summons me, I will answer. I also determined I would not deliberate or try to figure out in the natural what God was trying to do.

In light of recent events, there has been a lot of conflict concerning the election. The biggest question that needs to be answered is did the Prophets miss it? The short answer is no. That sounds insane because a President has already been inaugurated. Has it been a battle, unlike anything we have ever experienced, the answer would be yes? Has it turned out the way we expected? Not yet. How can you be so sure? I believe what God spoke to me. I have spent years learning to discern His voice and tune my ears to the frequency He speaks on. Therefore, when He speaks, I know it is Him. Did we get all the details? No. Do we think that God only speaks to known Prophets? Absolutely not. I Kings 18:19 says,

> *Nevertheless, I have reserved seven thousand in Israel— all whose knees have not bowed to Baal and whose mouths have not kissed him. (Berean Study Bible).*

On a phone call with some Nigerian women; one of them said, "The pandemic has unleashed demons in America that we have never had to fight." Also, we are excavating ancient demons that have ruled America for hundreds of years. Any person who has tried to remove a tree from their yard knows how deep the root systems can grow. The governing principle is if you kill the roots, you kill the fruit.

A BOTCHED ELECTION

God is after A Holy Nation with no leaven. Jesus spoke to the Fig Tree and the word says, "It withered from the roots" (Mark 11:20 NIV). Over a decade ago a Prophet asked the Lord why the sharks were coming in so close to the shore? And the Lord responded, "Because the hedge is lifting." So, as a Christian, have you been doing your part to keep the hedge lifted, or have you just been enjoying the benefits of being hedged?

It is also important to discern there is a difference between the carnal church and the remnant. The carnal church needs to understand what God is doing before they move. The remnant moves with God, whether they understand what He is doing or not. The long answer, which

A BOTCHED ELECTION

I will do my best to explain throughout the pages of this book; is what was prophesied came to pass. President Trump legally won the election, by a landslide.

I know this sounds far-fetched, but it is undeniably true and the coverup by the state governments has been unbelievable. It is crazy to me that people's lives have been threatened for coming forward. It feels like I am watching a movie. The nature of a landslide is that it sweeps everything in its path and then you have to go through the arduous task of digging things out.

I have put as many resource links as possible in the E-book to help you make an educated guess and to help you grow in the Prophetic. God is maturing the Prophetic Office and preparing them as His end-time army. This is the hour for God's Prophets to be fully informed and able to discern God's every move.

There was egregious Election and Voter Fraud in not just one state but several states. This is not about a political preference as much as it is about the truth. What God did not show us was the level of warfare that was going to ensue to undermine the Prophetic word. It shook the faith of even the most seasoned Prophets.

The Word admonishes us that we do not fight against flesh and blood therefore, this is the work of the enemy who sowed tares into the field. I believe part of the problem was the overwhelming assault of

COVID19 that was crippling this nation. It was everyone's focus, not the election.

Despite Satan's best shot, faith was birthed into the hearts of God's people as the drama began to ensue. I have never seen so much collective faith and Prophetic synergy in the hearts of so many people, both foreign and domestic, for this to be a strong delusion. God will have the final say-so and will uncover the truth for all eyes to see. I trust Him.

Looking at what we can see in the natural would give people the impression that the Prophets are making things up just to be right or we are all insane. But looking at the unseen ensures us that God has a plan so significant that the enemy

A BOTCHED ELECTION

unleashed an all-out assault against the Body of Christ. I heard a very credible Prophet say, "*Satan is trying to advance His agenda early but it is not yet His time.*" Daniel 7:25 says,

> *He will speak words against the Most High and try to exhaust the holy ones of the Most High. He will attempt to alter the seasons and the law; and [the holy ones] will be handed over to him for a time, times, and half a time (CJB).*

Make no mistake, the prophetic remnant, that has nothing to lose or gain, are still standing and are fully entrenched in battle. The victory belongs to the Lord because He has plans for America. God's prophetic army is moving in supernatural synergy. A nameless faceless army on stealth mode. As Executive Orders are being pushed out in lightning speed to erode the moral fiber of this nation, we must remember God's divine protection is completely surrounding us. Ask the Lord to favor you and open your eyes the way he did Elijah's servant. 2 Kings 6:15-17 (Berean Bible) says,

> *When the servant of the man of God got up and went out early in the morning, an army with horses and chariots had surrounded the city. So, he asked Elisha, "Oh, my master, what are we to do?" 16"Do not be afraid," Elisha answered, "for those who are with us are more than those who are with them." 17Then Elisha prayed, "O LORD,*

please open his eyes that he may see." And the LORD opened the eyes of the young man, and he saw that the hills were full of horses and chariots of fire all around Elisha....

This is not about a man as much as it is about the plan of God already scheduled on His agenda. President Trump being God's elected should remind you that you do not have to be perfect for God to use you. I will share later in the book why God shared with me one of the reasons He chose President Trump. He should be an inspiration to us all that God is not this evil judge waiting to slam the gavel and declare you guilty but instead, is a faithful Father executing your pardon.

A BOTCHED ELECTION

David was a man after God's own heart, and we know his story. God's design through the Bible was always to raise up deliverers who will execute His plan on the Earth. Ezekiel 22:30 says, *"I searched for a man among them to repair the wall and stand in the gap before Me on behalf of the land, so that I should not destroy it...* We see that in the lives of Moses, Deborah, Esther, Paul, Joshua and Jesus. As we navigate these prophetic waters ask God what is your next move?

The spirit of the living God is destroying the religious spirit that makes His people feel they do not measure up. Jesus said the letter of the law kills. Every prophetic word a person will ever get throughout their lifetime was already established at the point of conception. Psalms 139:15-16 (CJB) says,

> *My frame was not hidden from you, when I was being made in secret, intricately woven in the depths of the Earth. Your eyes saw my unformed substance; in your book were written, every one of them, the days that were formed for me, when as yet there was none of them.*

Every single day of a person's life is ordained by God, despite failures, broken relationships breached fellowship with the Holy Spirit, and sin. When we bear fruit worthy of repentance God knows how to navigate us through the rugged terrain of our lives and catapult us into the winds of destiny.

A BOTCHED ELECTION

Nothing is a surprise to Him. This was a hard-fought lesson for me.

If you are a Prophet that God spoke to be of good cheer and do not be dismayed or disheartened at the false narrative. Rest in the fact that you obeyed God and you did your part. The truth will prevail, it always does. The question we should be trying to answer is, "What is the enemy trying to stop?" Use the E-book to access the link and watch **Prophet** Kim Clements'i final video to America before He died.

A Change of Plans

On November 2, 2020, the day before the election, I was on my way to the Los Angeles Airport for a speaking engagement in Oklahoma City. As providence would have it, I never left the airport due to a mechanical issue with the airplane. God had other plans for me.

While in the airport I had several conversations with people regarding the presidential election.

Serendipitously we all had the same unction that God's hand was on President Trump. I want to make it clear that I am not knocking anyone who voted for Biden because everyone is entitled to vote for who they think is the best candidate; That is why we live in a free country.

    Once the airplane was repaired, six hours-later, I had a decision to make. The safest choice for me was to reschedule my trip because catching that plane would have left me in the Colorado Airport for two-days, which for me was not an option. When I arrived home, it was like I was slammed with the burden of the Lord to pray for the election.

A BOTCHED ELECTION

I saw a vision of a white horse (Revelations 6:1-2). I knew in the Spirit something was about to hit. The white horse represented those who would falsely come in His name and try to imitate Him, in essence, political and religious spirits pretend they are righteous and care about people but in their hearts is a seething diabolical plan.

The antichrist spirit does not want to be Christ. It only wants the glory and worship that belongs to Him and it will do anything to get it. This is being uncovered in the church and across the political landscape. The following evening, I went live on Facebook and began to pray for the election. This would last for over three months and at the time of writing this book, the burden has lifted and now I rejoice for the victory!

A Prophet said to me on September 25, 2020, in Springfield, Tennessee, "*You have had face to face encounters with demonic imps that have tried to take you out. You had a visitation in your bedroom (which I will elaborate on later) the enemy locked you down where you could not move or breathe.*

He sent a Python spirit to suffocate you. And the Lord has need of you for this new assignment that you are on. Your place of worship, prayer, and intercession will go to realms that you know not of."

I did not expect it to come so soon. The interesting thing was I was in Oklahoma City four years prior on the day President Trump was elected to his first term in 2016. I remember sitting at the table in Oklahoma City with some friends, I did not vote because I forgot my absentee ballot at home. Nor did I care about voting because both candidates, in my mind, were not viable. Hillary Clinton or Donald President Trump in office was frightening to me. When I heard Donald, President Trump won I was flabbergasted.

During dinner, another Prophet said that a picture of President Trump came up on her phone one night and God said, "He may not be the people's choice, but he is my choice." She said, "I know people are going to be mad at me, but I have to obey God." I heard the Holy Spirit say, "And he will do two consecutive terms." It stopped there, I never really thought about it again until two years later. God, over the next couple of years, started softening my heart towards President Trump and I started to pay attention to what he was doing and the changes he was making.

In mid-2018 two things happened. I did a video on Facebook entitled, "Did God Put President Trump in Office?" That did not go over well at all. People were livid at my suggestion, but I am never afraid of robust conversation because I think it is necessary, especially involving the Prophetic.

Then in April of 2018, I had a dream about a great revival that started breaking out in the church, specifically among the younger generation. While the revival was going on Russian soldiers stormed the church and everything that looked familiar disappeared, and the walls became bare and white. I started hiding everything that resembled any signs of Christianity. I hid the young people in the pockets within the building that now looked under construction.

I immediately got out of bed shaking and did a video called, The coming shift are you really a Christian?[ii] This particular dream would later make all the sense in the world to me. When I started hearing threats of socialism and communism in our nation through Black Lives Matter (BLM) and Antifa the Holy Spirit showed me the dream was a warning regarding the coming assault against the church. Socialism and Communism are not about a government take-over it is about worship. Hitler's face was plastered on every aspect of society.

The people in these false regimes want the people of this nation to worship them instead of the almighty who sits on the throne. Throughout this book, I will interject dreams and encounters with the Holy Spirit that I had over the course of 10 years that did not make sense to me up until now.

It is important to understand that prophecy is progressive you do not just get up one day and prophesy. God will deal with you for months and maybe even years regarding a matter. The First President Trump prophecy was reported in 1983; President Trump was around 37 years old in the early '80s and during several interviews, he started discussing his burden for the American economy. Many were asking him was he going to run for President and his response was always, "No, I enjoy what I am doing.

Then in 2008, Prophet Kim Clement, who died shortly after President Trump took office, started prophesying about him becoming President. A friend of mine was in the meeting with Kim Clement and said, she started laughing because it seemed so outlandish. Then in 2011, the Lord laid the same burden on then Fireman Mark Taylor, the author of the President Trump Prophecy[iii]. I also watched The Trump Card[iv] by Dinesh D'Souza which brought further clarity.

Initially, my first impression was there is something I did not know about everything that was going on. I try to do my research before I speak on a matter. I do not believe everything but follow the lesson of a very wise woman, who was the Dean of the college I attended. She always said, "Eat the meat and spit out the bones." Let me make it clear, I am not making a case for President Trump but for the anatomy of the Prophetic Word and Office.

God is very strategic in what He does and also takes His time until all things are in order and a matter enters into the fullness of time.

A BOTCHED ELECTION

Psalms 115:3 says, "*Our God is in heaven; he does whatever pleases Him.*" He can also choose who He wants without our permission. If we look at Biblical text the coming of Jesus was prophesied in the Garden of Eden, after Eve ate the forbidden fruit. Genesis 3:14-15 says, "

> *So, the LORD God said to the serpent: "Because you have done this, cursed are you above all livestock and every beast of the field! On your belly will you go, and dust you will eat, all the days of your life. And I will put enmity between you and the woman, and between your seed and her seed. He will crush your head, and you will strike his heel (NIV).*

A BOTCHED ELECTION

The Bible confirms that Jesus would arise out of the root of Jesse and rule over the Gentiles (Romans 15:12). Who was Jesse? Jesse was David's father. So, that tells me that God performed His Word and preserved His seed even through murder and adultery. God is not after perfection but agreement with His will and His plan. I Corinthian 1:27 says,

> *But God hath chosen the foolish things of the world to confound the wise; and God hath chosen the weak things of the world to confound the things which are mighty;* (KJV).

David was referred to throughout the Bible as, "*A man after God's own heart.*" Kim Clement said concerning President Trump, "*He *would not go into the office as a praying man, but he would come out of the office as a praying man."* Proverbs 21:1 reminds us, *"The king's heart is in the hand of the Lord, as the rivers of water: he turneth it whithersoever he will."*

The Church Is Awake

The enemy has tried to shut the mouth of the Church during this pandemic, but it backfired! The Church is now fully awake and engaged! Men and women of God, on every continent, have risen to the occasion. The George Floyd incident was used as a catalyst to usher in BLM, which is infuriating to me. Preying on the weakness of people and racial wounds is the work of the enemy. He is always looking for an opening to launch his felonious plans. The hypocrisy and level of evil are shocking to me. As we dig deeper into this matter, I want to remind you that the Word of God says in Ephesians 12:1 (NIV),

> *For our struggle is not against flesh and blood, but against the rulers, against the authorities, against the powers of this dark world, and against the spiritual forces of evil in the heavenly realms.*

This is not about who you like or do not like, and it is not about your personal opinion. It is about the fact that our nation is under siege, from within and without. Political experts are saying we are in the middle of a

A BOTCHED ELECTION

soft coup, meaning foreign nations are trying to take over our government and our people. These demonic entities want the soul of this nation to use for their malevolent agendas.

In 2008 a friend and I went and saw the movie Valkyrie. As we were walking out of the theatre, I felt something come over me that I could not explain. It was not an open vision it was just a weight. It was so overwhelming I went into the bathroom and had to sit down and weep. When I came out of the bathroom my friend asked me what happened because he said, "I looked different." The presence of the Holy Spirit was so heavy that my friend wept all the way to my home. Over the years this encounter faded from my memory.

I want to admonish you as a Prophet do not discount anything God shows you because somewhere in time the details are going to matter. True prophecy is a foretelling, and a true Prophet is an oracle of God saying only what He says. Remember I said that our nation is under a soft coup?

Then let me explain what the movie Valkyrie was about. Initially, Valkyrie was a Norse God who determined who died or lived in battle or the keeper of the slain. Many Political Analysts said where we are now reminds them of World War II and the reign of Hitler. Operation Valkyrie, the movie, was a military operation to overthrow Hitler and siege Germany.

While in prayer with Dutch Sheets' Appeal to Heaven Tour one of the Prophets had a dream called, "Valkyrie Will Fall and Not Sing^v" Hearing this made what I experienced in 2008 flood back. The Church launched operation Valkyrie, in the spirit, to take back our Nation from a Demonic coup. I believe the operation was successful and now we are waiting for God's final chess move. From a political standpoint, the Republican and Democratic parties no longer exist. Instead, we have been launched into the war of the ages.

As you read this book, I want to clarify some terms that have been thrown around in the news media. The term *"President Trump Supporters"* refers to religious conservatives or Christians. These are people that desire to continue the fight for freedom of religion and freedom of speech.

This group's purpose is to effect political agendas and public policy based on the teachings of Christ. This current regime is setting our nation up to persecute Christians, the writing is on the walls. Alex Stamos a disinformation expert in his CNN Interview [vi] believes it is their duty to shut down anyone that does not agree with their news and stifle free thinking. The term Radical Left refers to those who desire to push communism, Marxism, socialism, and other forms of anticapitalism. They want to continue their quest for wealth by sucking the Government dry, leave the people dependent and push an agenda that is completely against the Constitution and the Word of God.

As Christians, we can no longer haphazardly vote, we must vote for the Candidate that agrees with God's agenda and His Word. God is not a Democrat nor a Republican. The video by Pastor Gary Hamrick called, Church in America, Wake Up [vii] is the blueprint for voting for our Christian values and we must teach this to our children and grandchildren. We either do our part in advancing the work of Jesus or we open the floodgates for Satan's evil agenda against the people of God.

Holding the Line

There are four types of people who are reading this book. It is those who believe what the Prophets have declared, those who know they heard God's voice and believe this thing is not over, skeptics, and those who are wondering what the heck is going on? We must also lean on the nature of the one we serve. He is sovereign and reserves the right to execute His supreme power and authority. He is also about the redemption of His creation and is committed to truth and integrity. This thing looks so impossible and so did the crossing of the raging Red Sea, but the children of Israel made it over on dry ground.

Holding the line is a military term in which a line of troops was supposed to prevent an enemy breakthrough. Hold the line saints! endure the shaking, stand, and embrace the contradiction. This battle belongs to the Lord and I am on HIS side. All GOD needs is one night! He does not need days, months, or years to change anything. The Angel of the Lord killed 185,000 men in less than 24 hours; wiping out the entire Assyrian army while the people of God were asleep (2 Kings 19:35). If you are not sure what to do in this hour rest in Him, rejoice over the won battle, and continue to fulfill Purpose. Make God your place of peace, abide in HIS sanctuary, and praise Him for the victory. Revelations 12:11 says,

> *The saints of God overcame him by the blood of the Lamb and by the word of their testimony, and they loved not their lives unto the death (NIV).*

And Psalms 68:1-3 says,

> *May God arise, may his enemies be scattered; may his foes flee before him. As smoke is blown away by the wind, may you blow them away; as wax melts before the fire, may the wicked perish before God. But may the righteous be glad and*

rejoice before God; may they be happy and joyful (NIV).

Purifying the Prophetic Office

I want to address this issue not in relationship to the election but as a point of reference for prophetic ministry period. There are too many lone Prophets that have no credibility, no accountability, no Biblical foundation and no one that can vouch for their accuracy.

A BOTCHED ELECTION

In prayer, the Lord spoke to me regarding the contemporary Prophetic landscape. I believe one of the divine acts of God initiated through this election is the Draining of the Prophetic[viii] and political swamps. He is cleansing the church with a refiner's fire that will sweep through the pulpits and the pews. The money changers are being ejected and God is exposing financial and sexual corruption in the church.

The church as we know it will never be the same. There were several days where I had open visions of the swamp being incrementally drained. I saw it being completely drained and the plants were drying out. Once it was dry the bottom of it began to cave, and the final vision was the bottom of the swamp completely dropping out and opening up the portals of Hell. As we navigate through this book, we must understand Biblically that Hell is a choice (Isaiah 5:12-14). We are admonished to enter in through the narrow gate. Wide is the road that leads to destruction and narrow is the road that leads to eternal redemption (Matthew 7:13).

It is crucial to understand there are two types of Prophets named in the Bible: Prophets of God and False or Lying Prophets. The word of God says, *"If you would believe His Prophets you will prosper* (2 Chronicles 20:20), and the inverse is true. What do those, who declared and still believe what God said regarding President Trump's second term, have to gain? They have and are being ridiculed, while still standing in faith. Therefore, we have to determine are these Prophets, who have been credible for years, who prophesied and are still believing what God said is coming to pass delusional?

Or are the ones who are cowering under the pressure and apologizing right? First, Prophets of God only say what God says and False Prophets steal prophetic words from others and say what they think the people want to hear and blame it on God. There is no Biblical basis for Prophets apologizing. Apologizing, in my opinion, is merely an attempt to feign humility because they lost the fortitude to ride the thing out and what is more important to them is their personal ministry and not the Kingdom of God.

Prophets are not cut out for fame and nor is fame their portion or lot. Either you are a Prophet of Yahweh or a messenger of Satan. You either heard God or you did not. The word of God says in I Corinthians 13:19 (NLT),

> *"Now our knowledge is partial and incomplete, and even the gift of prophecy reveals only part of the whole picture*!

That is why Paul urged Timothy to wage a good warfare with the Prophetic words he received (I Timothy 1:18). Prophecy in Biblical text is progressively revealed. I Peter 2:19-20 declares,

We also have the word of the Prophets as confirmed beyond doubt. And you will do well to pay attention to it, as to a lamp shining in a dark place, until the day dawns and the morning star rises in your hearts. Above all, you must understand that no prophecy of Scripture comes from one's interpretation. For no such prophecy was ever brought forth by the will of man, but men spoke from God as they were carried along by the Holy Spirit... (Berean Bible).

Prophecy many times is like a relay race, you have the one who starts the race, runs the middle leg, and then the anchor. Maybe it was just your turn to pass the baton and you did not. God gives us faith for our part. I had no impression to pray for President Trump until November 3; although God had been speaking about it to me for two years. Albeit, some may have been holding the line for a while and got tired of the fight, but your response is not to apologize but to go get some rest. In World War II, the soldiers would get trench foot for being in the water too long and they had to get their feet out of the water for them to heal if healing were possible. Jesus pulled back from the crowd many times to replenish himself. Mark 6:31 (NIV) says,

> *Then, because so many people were coming and going that they did not even have a chance to eat, he said to them, "Come with me by yourselves to a quiet place and get some rest.*

Therefore, that would bring us to the question, there are a lot of Prophets speaking; but how can you be sure that their message is from God or for that matter their message is for you? The Prophetic has become a serve-yourself buffet and many presume they can just feast at any table. I believe the more access we have via Social Media, the more diluted and impotent the message becomes. Much of what is called prophecy is merely someone's opinion or a personal word that the Holy Spirit gave them.

I know when God is just speaking to me and when He is speaking to the masses. Mass messages are usually those that will affect a people group or a large geographical area. This is when we rely on the direction of the Holy Spirit. Most Prophets in the Bible lived a life of seclusion.

John the Baptist was one voice crying in the wilderness (John 1:23). Jesus often moved away from the crowd (Luke 5:16). Elijah single-handedly took down 450 Prophets of Baal (1 Kings 18:22); Which provides a framework that God does not move on the famous but inhabits those entrenched in the bastion of solitude that labor tirelessly to accurately hear His voice.

It is not notoriety that makes a Prophet effective but isolation and anonymity (I Kings 22:6-8). I heard a Prophet say, *"Prophets don't come out of the cave until God has something to say."* Our reliance, as believers, is on the God inside of us in the person of the Holy Spirit. You do not chase prophecy, prophecy chases you. Doing so is no different than reading your horoscope or visiting a psychic. New Testament prophecy is more confirmation than it is information.

Furthermore, The Holy Spirit said to me, "*The Prophetic has been contaminated with occultic practices (Deuteronomy 18:9-14).*" Very few discipline themselves to hear from God, crucify their flesh or drink from the well of revelation that flows from the Holy Spirit. Therefore, they have to rely on other sources to keep their ministries going and maintain their cash flow.

A BOTCHED ELECTION

God is purifying the Prophetic Office. Another issue is Prophetic training; I know the waters are murky. I pray that God will connect you to a healthy stream. No man can ordain you as a Prophet, from a Biblical perspective you are born one (Jeremiah 1:5). But you need to be trained on how to wield the Prophetic sword so that you do not cause more damage than good.

I heard a Prophet say, "It takes about 15 years to train a Prophet." And in my own life, this was true. I have been studying the Prophetic for about 30 years and set under a Prophet for 15 before I ever started moving in it. I believe this next season will be the exposition of the true nature and character of those that claim to speak in His name. Jeremiah 23:30-31 says,

> *Therefore," declares the Lord, "I am against the Prophets who steal from one another words supposedly from me. Yes," declares the Lord, "I am against the Prophets who wag their own tongues and yet declare, 'The Lord declares,(NIV).*

He is revealing those that do not have the Spirit of the Father but possess the spirit of Balaam and Gehazi. Balaam was a Prophet for hire; Balak presented to him a diviner's fee to curse the children of Israel and 2 Peter 2:15 (NIV) says,

> *They have left the straightway and wandered off to follow the*

way of Balaam son of Bezer, who loved the wages of wickedness.

Gehazi attempted to profit from Elisha's divine assignment. Naaman the Leper tried to bless Elisha for his Healing and Elisha's response was, *"As surely as the Lord lives, I will not accept a thing "* (2 Kings 5:16). But His servant Gehazi followed after Naaman and accepted the gift Elijah rejected. The penalty for accepting forbidden fruit was the same disease Naaman was healed from clung to Gehazi at the word of the Prophet. (2 Kings 5:27).

Many self-promoting and self-proclaimed Prophets today are chasing diviner's fees and filthy lucre (Numbers 22:7). Author Desiree

Mondesir said, "*That in the Prophetic, what you accept is what you become.*" It is not wrong to receive offerings nor be paid for what you do; giving is an established Kingdom dynamic to care for those that give themselves tirelessly to the gospel. I Corinthians 9: 13-14 admonishes us that,

> *Do ye not know that they which minister about holy things live of the things of the temple? and they which wait at the altar are partakers with the altar? Even so hath the Lord ordained that they which preach the gospel should live of the gospel (KJV).*

But that does not seem to be the case; these overzealous Prophets are bordering on heresy. They do not even preach from the scriptures, but from opinion and post-modernistic ideology; if it feels right, it is right. To see Cashapps plastered across Social Media everywhere is somewhat disturbing to me, is this what the church of Jesus Christ has come to? Are we money changers in the temple selling our wares?

A Liability to the Kingdom

One thing I have learned in life and through this election is that hurt dogs' holler. There are a lot of wounded Prophets in the camp; some justifiably and some still dealing with childhood trauma. Also, a lot of people have been offended and hurt by the Prophetic. It is critical in this season to be emotionally and spiritually healthy. A wounded

Prophet is a liability to the Kingdom of God. Much, if not all, of the unrest you see in our nation and our churches, is the revenge of the hurt. People spewing their childhood trauma on others.

A Prophet admonished me years ago, *"If you don't fix your limp, everyone you raise will have the same limp."* So, I have spent many years obeying that warning. There is a window of time that has been designated for the cleansing of the Prophets. Do not miss your moment! There is a mandate from Heaven that has been released; a supernatural grace for you to make your past truly your past. One of the best things that I ever did was submit to a year and a half of therapy to deal with my issues. I can honestly say the words from a song I love, *"I have dealt with my ghost and faced all my demons,"* is finally my story. If you need help get it, there is no harm or shame in that. We can no longer injure the Body of Christ by friendly fire and think that is okay.

God is dismantling every church or ministry that has partnered with the spirit that controlled Jezebel. The Lord is tired of seeing His people hurt and controlled by wounded Prophetic leaders. It does not mean the church or ministry may necessarily close down it means God will stamp ICHABOD (The Glory has departed) on the doors.

It will no longer be sanctioned by His Spirit but by the putrid and corrupt spirits of rebellious men and women who refuse to obey, heal, get help and repent. I heard a Prophet say, *"That God is the only boss who will fire you and let you keep working."* For those that do not heed the warning, *"His grace is being removed and they will now pay with their flesh. THE LORD SAYS, "My covering and protection is no longer available for them, but their souls will be saved."*

Now, this coming grace is available to release all offenses, roots of bitterness, crippling church wounds, abandonment, sexual abuse, verbal abuse, and rejection. Those things hurt, and they can scar us for life. But I stand in proxy for every person, parent, or spiritual leader that has hurt you. This is my declaration and call to repentance.

A BOTCHED ELECTION

From your perpetrator,

I want to ask you to forgive me for mishandling you, not acknowledging your anointing, inappropriately touching you, calling you names, making you feel like you did not matter, abandoning and rejecting you, ignoring your Prophetic call, controlling you, abusing you in any way because of your sex, your color, and your anointing. I declare that you are becoming everything God ordained you to be.

I decree God is now healing the wounds that cut so deep. I now release you into your Prophetic call. I affirm you, confirm you and call you my son or daughter. He put His stamp of approval on you when you were in your mother's womb and He called you from the foundations of the Earth to impact your generation. I declare you are entering into your due season and this will be your finest hour.

Raging in the Swing States

Close to 20 years ago I had a dream that I was walking down a long white corridor with a man that was finely-dressed and well-manicured. As we continued, I turned to him and asked, what is your name? With coal-black hair and deep blue-eyes, he said, "My name is America." A jolt of fear riveted my body…and then I woke up. What the Holy Spirit showed me about that dream recently was, as a nation we look amazing to the outsiders. Wealthy, beautiful, privileged, and bountiful but on the inside, we are possessed with every evil work. I heard a Prophet say, "*Powerful from without and weak from within.*" God wants to deal with that.

I read many years ago where someone had a dream that a red missile hit America and began to wreak havoc. I never forgot about that dream and would think about it over the years. We are in that time. I thought it was a literal missile but now understand it was the Coronavirus. When the Coronavirus first hit the Lord spoke to me very clearly and said this was demonic[ix], but He would use it for a greater purpose. God and the enemy can use the same event to fulfill their desired agenda, but it is God's plans that will always prevail.

When I saw an article that said, "Coronavirus Raging in the Swing States,"[x] I knew something was brewing. Why the swing states? Because it is not unusual that they flip between Democratic and Republican. God was using the pandemic to give His people rest. I heard a Prophet say that this, for the people of God, was a forced Sabbath.

He was resetting the table of family and of the Lord. He said to me personally, "*It was dark in Egypt and light in Goshen and that I and my family would want for nothing*", *(Exodus 10:23)*. Like a well-written movie, the enemy was going to use the pandemic and those that partnered with him to instigate one of the biggest election and voter fraud crimes in American history. Why? To move this nation into socialism, communism, and a one-world government.

Coronavirus was raging in the swing states because it would release fear on the people and open the door to massive mail-in ballots. I have gone through the arduous task of linking videos in the E-book. Of note some videos may have been taken down due to censorship. I encourage you to do your own research as well.

These threats by Cynthia Johnson who is a member of the Michigan House of Representatives from the 5th District were bone chilling. It let me know that this is a demonic ploy. Forgive the language but it is necessary to know what we are dealing with. I live in California, so my little Republican vote did not matter much. I have a gut instinct that California is no longer a Democratic state. But even in our state two-men tried to obtain 8,000 false mail-in ballots[xi]. The story was reported by Fox News on November 18, 2020.

You can also access Links to these stories in the E-Book

Biden and Harris owe Detroit.[xii]

Make the President Trumpers Pay[xiii]

Michigan Fraud Hearing[xiv]

A BOTCHED ELECTION

Sure, there has been election and voter fraud before but not on such a grand scale. The Gateway Pundit has reported for months now the fraud was extensive and historic. On Election night we went to sleep, and President Trump was winning by a significant amount in the swing states and was ahead in the Popular Vote.

They stopped counting. I have witnessed over eleven Presidential elections in my lifetime, and I have never seen one stop in the middle of the night, ever. The election was usually called that night except for The Bush versus Gore election where there was some discrepancy in Florida. That was one state, this election was several states. Which

A BOTCHED ELECTION

shows you the fraud was unprecedented.

We woke up and Biden was the most voted for President in American History. He even got more votes than Obama, which is highly and suspiciously unlikely. A man who has been in politics for 47 years and the only claim to fame in his political career is the Crime Bill[xv] which had a tremendous impact on the African-American Population and opened the door to mass incarceration. Biden later said, when preparing for the Presidential debate, the Crime Bill was a mistake.

Something was just not adding up. Then there is the issue of the Bell Weather Counties[xvi] who have almost always statistically chosen the

A BOTCHED ELECTION

Presidential candidate for closed 100 years. Many skilled and seasoned mathematicians have vehemently declared that Biden's win was statistically improbable.

I know people think that the election and voter fraud claims were a hoax, but Big Tech and Mainstream Media did everything they could to cover it up. On the backdrop of the election, thousands of people signed affidavits stating what they witnessed as well as testified at Senate Hearings under penalty of perjury. I will talk about the Prophets of Baal more extensively later. If it was legit then why do you need to censor people? I know people were censored and fact-checked because my page was affected as well.

A BOTCHED ELECTION

I am a Patriot and love my nation and know that we cannot stay here, or we will never have another fair election again. I have children and grandchildren that are American Citizens, and we have to clean it up for them. As a Prophet, you have a responsibility to govern your sphere of influence and establish the realm of God.

As part of our right as American citizens, we have a right to choose the people we want to run our nation. When we lose this, we will fall into the annals of socialism and communistic governments where we have no right to choose. That was Satan's plan, but it is not God's plan. God is the ultimate ruler of this nation and we are under His government. You are a watchman over the affairs of the Kingdom. You no longer have the right to be ignorant about what is going on in our nation.

The global church of Christ is depending on you to man your prophetic post! You do not need someone to tell you, you are released, ordain you or permit you to operate in the gift God gave you. God has released you in your sphere of influence. What if Jesus said He did not want to get involved, where would we all be? He confronted the religious heresy and political corruption of his day.

The Black Lives Matter Agenda

June 2020 changed everything for me. I had never seen such chaos and anarchy in my life. What I initially thought was the mark of something good ended up being the beginning of something that was trying to fundamentally change America as we know it. I was grateful to see that the racism that had plagued our nation for centuries was being dismantled but the people who initiated this movement did not care about African-American people, their concern was to push their own agenda using a pain-point and weakness in our American History. Manipulators will always capitalize on wounds. BLM is a leftist organization that violates our basic Christian beliefs.

The real agenda of BLM is the advancement of the Marxist Government that wants to destroy the basic foundation of the nuclear family. These are spirits that want to control people and rob them of the liberty that Christ died for. These spirits oppose God and are antichrist. BLM was merely a front for George Soros who many say is on a quest to destroy America. He financially backs several leftist and open-society organizations whose desire is to destroy the internal fabric of this nation through his Demonic agenda. The co-founder of BLM Patrisse Cullors said in an interview with Jared Ball, "*We are trained Marxists. We are super-versed on, sort of, ideological theories. And I think that what we really tried to do is build a movement that could be utilized by many, many black folks*,"

One of the things I teach Prophets is, it is important to have a Biblical World View. So, what does that mean? It means that the truth of the Bible is the foundation of everything you believe and determines how you engage with the world around you. There are so many philosophies out there that contradict our doctrine of faith. I am convinced that part of the confusion in the Prophetic is the lack of scriptural acumen. 2 Timothy 3:16-17 (NIV) says,

> *All Scripture is God-breathed and is useful for teaching, rebuking, correcting, and training in righteousness, so that the servant of God may be thoroughly equipped for every good work.*

So, why is this important? It is important because I am intertwining a thread to show how many events are weaved into a Prophetic word. We do not prophesy in a silo. There are so many factors in the accuracy of a Prophetic word. The Word of God says we prophesy in part. The

A BOTCHED ELECTION

Greek translation of the word part means portion or share. God does not show any one person the entire picture, every Prophet has a portion which means collective prophecy is crucial. The Prophetic is not a one-man show and God is no longer going to allow it to be exploited.

If we look at the prophecy of Jesus' birth and ministry there were so many events and factors that had to take place until the fulness of time was reached. Satan will always intervene in the plan of God which means attack the prophetic word. He is privy to Kingdom information because He is an angelic being whose abode was once in Heaven. Job 1:6-7 says,

A BOTCHED ELECTION

One day the sons of God came to present themselves before the LORD, and Satan also came with them. "Where have you come from?" said the LORD to Satan. "From roaming through the Earth," he replied, "and walking back and forth in it (NIV).

The sons of God derive from the Hebrew phrase, *bene Elohim*, which is an indication that these beings were part of God's divine judicial counsel. Satan, who was a fallen angel, was looking for information he could use against the people of God to render an accusation. He is always running interference.

A BOTCHED ELECTION

One strategy that I have tucked under my belt, concerning the Prophetic, is whatever I see the enemy doing I know that God is doing the opposite. Satan is a counterfeit and will always be. Joseph told his brothers during the famine in Egypt, *"You intended to harm me, but God intended it for good to accomplish what is now being done, the saving of many lives"*, (Genesis 50:20).

As we move forward it will befit us to fully research an organization before we hop on the train. What seems good is not always good and what appears to be right is not always right. BLM was just a smokescreen for the Radical Left to further their agenda.

The Prophets of Baal

The modern-day Prophets of Baal are Big Tech, Fact Checkers, PolitiFact, and The Associated Press (AP). PolitiFact and Fact-Checkers are independent organizations that think they have the right to verify what people are saying online. When I questioned Facebook about their credentials no response was given. The AP was the one who reported Biden as President-Elect while he was still a private citizen, which he technically was until January 6. Never in the history of our country has a News Paper had the authority to call an election before it was over. They were off to the races to start inculcating the people's minds with false information.

They have joined forces to report news that pushes their agenda rather than the unbiased truth. Unfortunately, their agenda is the Radical Left, everything that God hates. The goal is to influence public opinion by unleashing false narratives. They started suspending people's accounts, taking people's videos down on YouTube, bleeping the word "fraud," demonetizing people's platforms to silence those that contradicted their agenda. One of the up and coming Social Media

A BOTCHED ELECTION

sites, called Parler[xvii], was removed from the Google and Apple App Store. Amazon also removed them off of their server for "inciting a riot." The real truth is that people were leaving these Social Media platforms by the droves and Parler was becoming a threat to Big Tech. I think it is time to go back to old-fashioned face-to-face communication and Christian fellowship.

These news giants plastered their evil propaganda about the election and Coronavirus all over YouTube with banners under every video. CNN recently admitted, through video shared by Project Veritas, it was their job to destroy Trump and get him out of office. There next assault will be Climate Control so they can make these green companies push their false and financial agendas. Ironically, they can fill the airways with lies but everyone else is forbidden to speak and share their opinion, especially concerning the 2020 Election.

When I went to run an ad on Instagram for this book it was declined. Instagram's response was, "*This information can sway public opinion.*" The question I would ask is, "*Isn't the Election over?*" I am not sure if I will even be able to print it on Amazon for the same reason, as they have joined the party. Is not this the same tactic that Hitler used to take over Germany and kill thousands of innocent people? Where is the respect for our First Amendment Right of Free Speech. This is what separates us from every other country in the world, our ability to express our own opinions and be free-thinkers.

I started watching One American News Network, and Epoch News who are independent news networks, because of the coverage they were doing for Christians. A report said, "*This battle is the classic war between good and evil.*" When I saw what Social Media and the AP were reporting I was appalled at the obvious disparity and incongruity.

They would block the President of the United States but leave a video up of a child being violated. Twitter's response was concerning the child video, "*It did not violate their policy.*" We may not agree on the election but one thing I know for sure is the real battle is to save our babies.

My Facebook page did not get censored until I posted an article written by Breitbart on Pornhub. The message Facebook sent me was, "*Someone reported your page, we are trying to keep your group safe.*" The real question is what is their agenda and whose side are they on? I am so grateful we have access to the Holy Spirit who exposes the truth.

The Prophets of Baal and the Goliaths of our day have emerged hurling lies, baseless empty threats, and accusations to bring fear and intimidation. Their main objective is to silence the voice of God and the Prophets. Social Media has been a tremendous way to spread the

Gospel in a matter of seconds. That is why we must fight all the more. But as Prophets of God, we do not fear, David took Goliath down in a single blow. Prophetic information is God's prayer list.

Now let us talk about the witches. During President Trump's first term I saw several articles online that indicated witches were joining alliances to curse his presidency. In October 2020 this article was released by the US Sun, "*SPELLING IT OUT Thousands of witches plotting to cast 'binding spell' on Donald President Trump on Halloween so he loses to Biden on election day.*" The witches joined forces to get Joe Biden elected. The Holy Spirit also led me to the hashtag #witchthevote.

I saw a video of them on Instagram laying their hands in prayer on the Clark County Registrars Building in Nevada to curse the vote. The caption said, *"You are praying, and we are putting in work too."* Prophets it is time to engage in battle!

It is horrifying to me that witches are more organized than the Body of Christ. And one thing I know for sure is Satan does not attack his own. Even Jesus was called an insurrectionist operating under the power of Satan. Anything or anyone that opposes Satan's plan will be labeled as a trouble-maker. Matthew 12:24-25, concerning Jesus, says,

> *But when the Pharisees heard this, they said, "It is only by*

A BOTCHED ELECTION

Beelzebub, the prince of demons, that this fellow drives out demons." Jesus knew their thoughts and said to them, "Every kingdom divided against itself will be ruined, and every city or household divided against itself will not stand (NIV).

The Prophets of Baal highly publicized the February 6 event to further rip the fabric of our nation. We see utter chaos and anarchy at the Capital to stop the states in question from contesting the Electoral Votes. Rep Paul Gosar and Senator Cruz challenged Arizona's results. It is clear that Antifa was involved, and many were arrested with little News Paper coverage, they were just continuing the work they were doing in Portland. You do not hear anyone from the Left discussing the chaos in that region that has been going on for months.

Following the Capital Building storming the others that were going to contest the electoral votes backed down. Evil prevailed again, mission accomplished. Before the incident at the Capital, Maricopa County in Arizona received a Subpoena, which was ignored by the county, until after the Electoral College votes were confirmed, to review their voting machines. Certifying Electoral votes that are not valid is a punishable crime.

As we speak, Arizona and several other states are in the process of trying to conduct forensic audits on the election to determine the level of fraud. In Arizona, the Supreme Court determined that the Board of Supervisors actions are illegal and unconstitutional and demanded they release the Ballots and machines for a forensic audit. The Board of Supervisors, at the time this book was published are still defying the judge's verdict and obstructing justice.

The people in the county are already convinced there was fraud they just want to know how much? The results of this audit can potentially flip the entire election. The Board of Supervisors in Arizona are still resisting the Subpoena. Why? What is there to hide?

Texas officials stated there were too many vulnerabilities with the Dominion Voting Machines and therefore refused to use them. Michigan had an issue stating 6,000 votes for President Trump were inadvertently given to Biden. Where there is smoke there is fire. In this case a raging unquenchable forest fire.

In 2019 NBC reported, "How hackers can Target Voting Machines." As a Democratic Nominee Biden recorded a video, in order to defraud the American people, and said "*We have created the most extensive and inclusive voter fraud organization in the history of American politics.*"

Which we now know was not true. It also tells us that the Leftist have been planning this for a long time. President Trump just got in their way. Their next move was Hillary Clinton.

The Christian organizations that were in support of the Capital on that day were Stop the Steal, which was banned by Facebook, The Jericho March, amongst other God-fearing Christians. Why are people being censored? The answer is to cover the truth. The MSM are banning and censoring, anything that resembles justice and Christianity. We are in an hour where the Bible must be written upon the tablets of our hearts now.

What I know in the end is the truth will prevail and God is a man of justice for His name's sake. We know ultimately that this is not about a man or an election but about the plan of

God that the enemy is trying to stop. A quote said,

> *"We are dealing with an Antichrist spirit they don't want to get rid of God they want the worship God gets. People appear to be doing what's right in public but working the works of darkness in private. Gaslighting those that are righteous to make them seem wicked so they can draw attention away from themselves."*

It is the classic Wizard of Oz scenario, a small feeble man, manipulating people to believe his lies.

The Nature of This Battle

The nature of this present battle is against political and religious demons that want to remain in control. James Goll said, "*The **political spirit** is an invisible demonic mastermind that strategizes ways to thwart God's plans; to achieve its corrupt goals, it enters into alliances with religious **spirits** and institutions often backed by mammon.*"

A BOTCHED ELECTION

Jesus' main fight was with the Sadduceeic and Pharisaic leaders that were threatened by His divine entrance. They knew they could not stop the roar of the lion of the tribe of Judah and could not neutralize the supremacy of the new regime and Kingdom.

These spirits operate the same; It is to make the masses obey the few. This is a modern-day Showdown on Mount Carmel. Jesus said, *"Take heed, beware of the leaven of the Pharisees and the leaven of Herod."* (Mark 8:15 says). Roberts Liardon said, "*A religious spirit is so dangerous making people think they are serving God and they are not.*" The root of these spirits is the lust for power and jealousy. God took Ezekiel in the temple and He saw at the altar the seat of Jealousy (Ezekiel 8:5). The reason jealousy is so dangerous is it is one of the things that got Satan kicked out of Heaven (Isaiah 14:13). Therefore, when someone is jealous of you all the powers of Hell are unleashed against you.

On May 22, 2020, two days before George Floyd was murdered, I had a demonic encounter with a religious spirit in the form of a Bishop dressed in all his vestments. He was bigger than life and not the normal size of a human, the Spirit was restraining me and the more I struggled to be free the more breath began to leave my body. And I remember crying out, "I can't breathe." The fear that gripped my heart was unlike anything I had experienced in recent times. In

A BOTCHED ELECTION

September, as previously mentioned, a Prophet in Nashville addressed that very encounter and said, "*It was because God was preparing me for a new assignment.*" An assignment that God had been grooming me for, for several months.

God is using me, and other Prophets, to set the people free from the bondage of religious rules and regulations and political spirits that use control and manipulation to invoke fear in the people. Religion has destroyed the masses and made people feel like they are not acceptable to God unless they are perfect. It has also harassed the Prophetic anointing and labeled some as witches to silence the voice of God in the church. The political spirit has hijacked the church to tell them what they can preach and what they cannot. When they can open and when they cannot. How to worship and how not to worship.

During hours of intercession, I realized, at some point, the conflict had escalated to the realm of principalities and powers. It is rulers of regions and countries that do not want to leave the place in which they have domiciled for so many years. When Jesus had the conversation with Legion, it was not about if he was coming out; because that was settled. The discussion was where he was going because he did not want to leave the region. Mark 5:8-10 says,

> *For Jesus had already declared, "Come out of this man, you unclean spirit!" "What is your*

name?" Jesus asked. "My name is Legion," he replied, "for we are many." And he begged Jesus repeatedly not to send them out of that region....

There are political and religious demons that have ruled this country for centuries. The spirit of mammon has been unleashed in the world and the church. The pursuit of gain and wealth at all costs has been the quest of many. I decree that America is being cleansed.

An unnoticed manifestation of a religious spirit is mental illness. Mark 5:15 says (NIV),

> *When they came to Jesus, they saw the man who had been possessed by the legion of*

A BOTCHED ELECTION

demons, sitting there, dressed and in his right mind; and they were afraid.

I have never seen so many Christians bound by anxiety and medication. If you are, for a season, there is no shame; but as blood-bought believers, we have dominion and authority over the Devil and his torment. God is resurrecting dominion power in the church and the enemy is afraid of Saints in their right minds.

Prophets this is the hour to engage in warfare for this nation and your destiny. There is no more grace to stand on the sidelines and watch things happen, it is time to declare and decree things that you know God wants to happen. The grace has been released to take your rightful place on the frontline and let the high praises of God be in your mouth and a two-edged sword in your hand (Psalms 149:6). Take authority and speak those things which be not as though they were. If you do not know what to pray; speak the word of God that you know to be true and ask the Holy Spirit what your portion is.

My home state of California has been hit the hardest and is under direct assault because of the revivals that have come out of this region and swept eastward. We were told we could not sing, play instruments, or pray in public or our homes. The. Azusa street revival of 1910, which was a multi-ethnic and multi-gender revival gave birth to the modern Pentecostal and Charismatic movements in the 20th Century. Amie Semple-McPherson dropped her mantle in Oakland, California. The Jesus Movement of the late '60s and early '70s unlocked the Prophetic movement and Apostolic Reformation that is still present today.

A political analyst said that this same assault happened in our nation during the early '70s. According to the FBI, there were 2500 bombings, about five a day by a Radical Leftist group. He said the movement fizzled out because the church was too strong. Let us get back to it and assume the position.

Revenge or Revival

So, what is God after, and what is Satan trying to stop? During the riots, the Lord began to speak to me, and I understood that this was a watershed moment in American history, of the likes we have never seen. So, what is this all about? And what does this have to do with the election? It will all make sense soon. Although the George Floyd murder and the crime of police brutality are the catalysts, or the tipping point it is so much deeper. I am in no way minimizing what has happened, but I also do not want to ignore that something more is brewing under the surface. Please continue to pray for George Floyd's family and declare that justice will be served.

The blood of innocent people is crying up from the ground and God is ready to avenge the atrocities of slavery, abortion, human trafficking of children, church abuse, and Prophets for profit. He is also disarming religious and political spirits that are choking the life out of people who desire to meet a God that this nation claims to intimately know.

The blood is still speaking today, and the cry of the people has reached the ears of God. Hebrews 11:4 says,

> *By faith Abel brought God a better offering than Cain did. By faith he was commended as righteous, when God spoke well of his offerings. And by faith Abel still speaks, even though he is dead.*

Jesus spoke to the religious leaders of His day and provoked their religious and political piety by saying,

> *Therefore. this generation will be held responsible for the blood of all the Prophets that has been shed since the beginning of the world, from the blood of Abel to the blood of Zechariah, who was killed*

between the altar and the sanctuary. Yes, I tell you, this generation will be held responsible for it all, (Luke 11:50-51 Berean Bible).

What we see happening in the Earth is a shaking in the spirit. We cannot force ourselves to believe that we serve a God who turns His face on the carnage currently taking place. Although I am grateful that I was born in this nation, I also am one who contends for authentic revival and true Christianity. The Apostle Paul admonished the church in Corinth,

What agreement has the temple of God with idols? For we are the temple of the living God; as God said, "I will make my dwelling among them and

walk among them, and I will be their God, and they shall be my people. Therefore, go out from their midst, and be separate from them, says the Lord, and touch no unclean thing; then I will welcome you. (2 Cor. 6:16-17, NIV).

If the church mimics the world, then what good are, we? If we are biting and devouring one another what purpose are we serving? I believe we are entering one of the greatest ages the church has ever experienced. Therefore, it is necessary and required that all hands be on deck to participate in one of the greatest revivals the world has ever experienced. The Third great awakening is upon us. Jude urged the saints (Jude 1:3, NIV),

A BOTCHED ELECTION

Dear friends, although I was very eager to write to you about the salvation we share, I felt compelled to write and urge you to contend for the faith that was once for all entrusted to God's holy people.

Hence, I ask you, in the wake of everything that has transpired is God after revenge or revival?

Praying For the President

In 2008 Prophet Kim Clement Prophesied there would be two Presidents and two Inaugurations. It reminds me of the story of Adonijah and his brother Solomon. David promised Bathsheba that Solomon would be King (I Kings 1:15-17), but Adonijah decided to inaugurate himself. One legitimate and the other illegitimate. I Kings 1:9 (NIV) says,

A BOTCHED ELECTION

Adonijah then sacrificed sheep, cattle, and fattened calves at the Stone of Zoheleth near En Rogel. He invited all his brothers, the king's sons, and all the royal officials of Judah, but he did not invite Nathan the Prophet or Benaiah or the special guard or his brother Solomon.

Adonijah did not invite the people that could vouch for the legitimacy of his pursuit; his father's Prophetic counsel, his father's chief counsel, the priest, nor the special guard to his brother Solomon because they knew He was illegitimate. During Adonijah's fake inauguration Solomon was being anointed King by Zadok the Priest and Nathan the Prophet. 1 Kings 1:32 – 35, (NIV) says,

> *King David said, "Call in Zadok the priest, Nathan the prophet and Benaiah son of Jehoiada." When they came before the king, he said to them: "Take your lord's servants with you and have Solomon my son mount my own mule and take him down to Gihon. 34There have Zadok the priest and Nathan the prophet anoint him king over Israel. Blow the President Trumpet and shout, 'Long live King Solomon!' Then you are to go up with him, and he is to come and sit on my throne and reign in my place. I have appointed him ruler over Israel and Judah.*

A BOTCHED ELECTION

These offices were ordained and sanctioned to confirm the work of God on the Earth. It is not whether we want to believe it or not, or we like it or not, it is a Biblical mandate that does not change based on man's opinion. God will always choose a deliverer when there is a matter on His agenda that needs attention. He will not consult with a man for approval.

Concerning this inauguration, some things seemed very odd. Too many inconsistencies in the natural should alert you that something is out of sync in the spiritual realm. The Bible declares on Earth as it is in Heaven (Matthew 6:10). To the Prophetic discerning eye, the disarray is not God's nature.

Order is a byproduct of legitimacy. Corinthians 15:46 says, *"The spiritual did not come first, but the natural, and after that the spiritual."* In the natural Biden was sworn in 12 minutes earlier than the constitutional Noon departure of the former President. Constitutionally it was no big issue, but it was a sign that something was out of order at the start. It just seems like this administration is in such a rush to get things done, which sounds like the enemy to me because he knows his time is short.

Another anomaly is the White House was locked upon Biden's Arrival. Also, Kamala and her husband are still unable to move into the Vice-President's quarters due to repairs. At the time, this books is being published, and two months into her tenure as Vice President she still has not moved in.[xviii] Something is off. I believe that Mike Pence is undergoing spiritual renovation. I believe he is a man of God.

Then there is the awkward two-minute unexplainable silence during the inauguration. During the silence, a baby cried. Prophet Robin Bullock said, "*The blood of the babies was crying up from the ground.*" When Biden broke his foot the Holy Spirit asked me what does the foot represent? I said authority. God told Joshua "*I will give you every place where you set your foot, as I promised Moses* (Joshua 1:3)." His broken foot to me was a sign that there was no divine authority for him to take that position.

One pastor warned Joe Biden, *"Be careful about touching the Ark by laying your hand on the Bible and drafting Executive Orders that are violating the very premise of what the Bible stands for."* Uzziah touched the Ark wrong and dropped dead. He violated God's protocol and his response to the Ark was illegal. The Ark was laid in the house of Obed-Edom and was unable to be touched for three months.

There is too much Prophetic synergy for things to be coincidental. When we judge a President, we judge them by what is put on paper, not their personality. Biden's first few days have moved this nation towards his socialistic agenda and the continued killing of the unborn, as well as the forward advancement of the LGQBT political agenda. I am not talking about those struggling with homosexuality, I believe an anointing is coming from Heaven to heal people, that want to be free from this lifestyle. I know this nation is not perfect and as an African-American woman, I acknowledge the egregious nature of slavery, bigotry, and racism.

But as a Christian, I am part of another Kingdom where there is no racism or schism because of natural differences. When I accepted Christ and was washed in His blood it made me a new creature and my worth in the Kingdom has nothing to do with the color of my skin.

A BOTCHED ELECTION

The reason I cannot pray for Biden is that he is not God's choice and he has made willful decisions that have proven to be wicked; wickedness is a choice. Because this was a stolen election with confirmed foreign interference it was an intentional effort to deceive the people and rob them of their choice. People started praying for Biden before President Trump was illegally put out of the office which is a direct violation of scriptures.

Our prayers are for the seated President legally elected by the people. Because there was no Prophetic agreement and Biden was illegally set in place, He is not the seated President. The Bible does not tell us to pray for the wicked. He said in Psalms 92, the wicked (twisted, unjust, schemers of evil) will be cut off. Proverbs 2:22 (ESV) says, "*but the wicked will be cut off from the land, and the treacherous will be rooted out of it.*" I can pray for his soul as a man but not for him as the legal President of the United States.

Again, I want to reiterate that I believe all this is about sex-trafficking and the crime against the unborn. The Lincoln Project's aim during the 2020 presidential election was to prevent the re-election of Donald President Trump and defeat all Republicans in close races running for re-election in the United States Senate. The co-founder, John Weaver, was accused of sexual misconduct. Pedophilia and sexual harassment. These are wicked evils that rob people of their God-given destiny. Then there is the other issue of God's relationship with Israel. Genesis 12:23 was God's promise to Abraham and his descendants,

> *And I will make you a great nation, And I will bless you, and make your name great; And so, you shall be a blessing; And I will bless those who bless you, And the one who curses you I will curse. And in you, all the families of the Earth will be blessed. (NASB)*

I know there is a lot of doctrine going around about the Black Israelites but for the sake of continuity, I will not debunk or affirm this movement. I do understand false religion is always the result of disenfranchisement and the revenge of the hurt. As a Biblical Christian God has always had a special relationship with Israel. Jesus was God's response to save His people, bring them into His agenda, and graft us into the vine. in 2017 President Trump globally acknowledged the city of Jerusalem as the capital of Israel and also initiated The Abraham Accord which was an unprecedented peace agreement in the Middle East. These strategic moves by the President are the heart of our Heavenly father.

The Advancement of Evil

If there has ever been a time to pray the hour is now, the soul of our nation is at stake the enemy has swung this election so that the Homosexual Agenda can be further advanced in this nation through The Equality Act that will now make it illegal for us to discriminate against them. They can teach in our Christian Schools, which they will. They can get married in our Christian Churches, which they will. Although they are few, they have made themselves mighty by attaching themselves to the Civil Rights Agenda. Biden is at a fever pitch advancing the LQBTQ agenda.

Also, this is the 50th anniversary of Roe vs. Wade. A woman's right to kill her unborn child. This bill is especially egregious to me because I had an abortion when I was younger believing the lie. If you have had an abortion and are still struggling with the shame and guilt of it, I command you to be free and released. A Prophet said God showed him, *"There were three principalities that were standing on the White House contending for this nation. They were racism, the God of Molech, and radical feminism.*" He said all three of those were connected to Planned Parenthood's founder Margaret Sanger.

Her agenda was to annihilate unborn black babies, in essence, Genocide. Genocide is, "*The deliberate killing of a large number of people from a particular nation or ethnic group with the aim of destroying that nation or group.*" In this hour we must burn for what is righteous and make the decision about whose side we are on. When Joshua was nearing Jericho, he encountered an angel and asked him are you for us or against us? The angel replied, "No, I am on the Lord's side (Joshua 5:13-14).

A BOTCHED ELECTION

I remember early in my walk there was a Planned Parenthood opening up in my neighborhood and the Holy Spirit instructed me to walk around that building every morning and uproot its evil agenda and I obeyed. That office never opened and stood vacant for a couple of years and was then torn down. The majority of Planned Parenthoods are put in minority neighborhoods for a reason. Biden is doing everything he can to keep this atrocity going by funding global abortion.

Interestingly, Mary Coney Barrett was elected to the Supreme Court in this hour – She believes in the sanctity of life. I believe it is a sign to the nations that the color of your skin should not determine the quality of your life. This is the season of first in American Politics; She is the first judge ever sworn in before the election. Was it a ploy by President Trump to push his agenda or was it, God's plan? I first knew God elected him, when I heard him say, "*The most important job of a President is to set the supreme court.*" The Supreme Court will have to answer to God. We must remember that God is in control and He holds the very breathe we breath. No human being is beyond His power.

I also believe this is the Spirit of Jezebel and she is trying to shut the mouths of the Prophets. This is the hour of a showdown on Mount Carmel where Elijah massacred Jezebel's Prophets. COVID19 is very real but it is also a smokescreen for Satan to push his evil agenda and advance it prematurely. We are not voting for a president we are contending for the soul of this nation for our children, grandchildren, and great-grandchildren.

WHAT WE DECREE

We decree that God releases judgment on the wicked.

We decree that the people's choice will be honored.

We decree that all deception and Satan's diabolical assignment be exposed.

We decree evil men who are trying to tamper with the voting practices be uncovered.

A BOTCHED ELECTION

We decree that the unborn will have a voice and Roe vs. Wade will be overturned.

We decree the end of systemic racism and oppression for people of color.

We decree the removal of all elected officials that are operating under deception.

We decree the church to be refreshed, replenished, and renewed.

We decree the freedom to worship the God of Abraham, Isaac, and Jacob.

We decree the abolishment of systemic racism, liberty, and freedom for all nationalities.

A BOTCHED ELECTION

Why Did the Prophets Miss It?

Maturing The Prophetic

Prophecy for most people today is just confirmation of something they want. A true Prophetic word is a future event that demands several responses. It requires agreement, obedience, and an act of faith. Prophecy is not fortune telling or psychic readings. What has happened to the Body of Christ is that we do not know how to contend with a word so when it does not go the way we think we lose hope and think the Prophets missed it.

It is important to remember that God lives outside of time and Earthly laws. He is not bound to this Earth system and does everything from the throne room. A true Prophetic word cares nothing about our feelings or what we think; its only objective is to work out all things according to the counsel of His own will (Ephesians 1:11).

I want to add that prophecy is not trying to move the hand of God and make Him do something that He has not purposed. Moving the hands on a clock does not change the time. It is, in essence, coming into spiritual synergy to see what He planned to manifest in the Earth realm. Everything we see in the Earth realm has already been established in Heaven (Matthew 6:10).

The Prophetic ministry is no longer in its infancy stage it is maturing. You are going to need more than a casual word, you are going to need intelligence, anointing, and natural agreement. We are now the frontline and the foot soldiers in the Body of Christ. The stakes in America are higher and people have infiltrated this country that hate us and hate the God we serve. The warfare has risen to another level and is at a fever pitch.

As Prophetic people, we are required to engage in every aspect of society. History is our greatest teacher; The Black Robe Regiment were British men of God who threw off their sacred clergy garments to storm the front line in prayer. Below are a couple of quotes from the National Black Robe Regiment website,

> *If Christian ministers had not preached and prayed, there might have been no revolution as yet – or had it broken out, it might have been crushed. [7] Bibliotheca Sacra [BRITISH PERIODICAL], 1856*

> *The ministers of the Revolution were, like their Puritan predecessors, bold and fearless in the cause of their country. No class of men contributed more to carry forward the Revolution*

A BOTCHED ELECTION

and to achieve our independence than did the ministers. . . . [B]y their prayers, patriotic sermons, and services [they] rendered the highest assistance to the civil government, the army, and the country. [8] B. F. Morris, HISTORIAN, 1864

Concerning the election prophecy, it is not about a person it is about God's plans and purposes. He planned to redeem the house of Israel, so He created a body in the person of Jesus (Hebrews 10:5). The people did not reject God's plan, they rejected Jesus; the person will always come under contradiction.

The same is with you; God created a body for you to fulfill your purpose because a spirit cannot operate in the Earth realm legally. So, some people like you and some do not but that does not neutralize God's purpose for your life. God told Jeremiah,

> *Before I formed you in the womb, I knew you, before you were born, I set you apart; I appointed you as a Prophet to the nations.* (Jeremiah 1:5, NIV)

The operative word is *"Before"* We can never allow ourselves to deliberate over who God chooses because it is His choice, not ours and He is not at the discretion of our opinion. Psalms 115:3 says, *"Our God is in heaven; he does whatever pleases him."*

A BOTCHED ELECTION

How do you know a Prophetic word is true? From experience, God speaks on a specific frequency and as a Prophet, you have to discipline yourself to hear God's voice through prayer, fasting, worship, and most importantly studying the scriptures. You cannot unhear a Prophetic word just like you cannot unborn a baby. I know that may not be good English, but the implications are weighty. When God speaks to me, I know it is Him because that voice is familiar to me. Even the Prophet Samuel had to get familiar with hearing God's voice. Samuel 3:7-9 (NIV) says,

> *Now Samuel did not yet know the Lord: The word of the Lord had not yet been revealed to him. A third time the Lord called, "Samuel!" And Samuel*

got up and went to Eli and said, "Here I am; you called me. So, Eli told Samuel, "Go and lie down, and if he calls you, say, 'Speak, Lord, for your servant is listening...

Most of today's Prophetic ministry is merely a regurgitation of something someone else said. The prophetic discipline is at an all-time low because people are chasing money not Glory.

As a Prophet, you cannot only read devotionals, sing worship songs, watch videos, listen to podcasts, and go to church. You are going to have to spend some time barricaded in the presence of God and the Word of God so you can get accustomed to the frequency in which He speaks.

A BOTCHED ELECTION

I know my children's voices but sometimes my daughters can sound the same; If that can happen in the natural it can happen in the Spirit. Another thing I learned about the Prophetic is when God speaks to you about a matter it reverberates and marinates in your spirit until the matter in you is settled. God's word is already settled in Heaven, we have to settle it on Earth.

Also, we do not prophesy in a silo, there has to be an agreement in the Earth that confirms what God is doing. Both through natural signs and other credible Prophetic voices. For me, dreams I did not understand, over the past twelve years have made complete sense now.

A BOTCHED ELECTION

The Prophetic word also runs along the continuum of time and too many people have had dreams, visions, and Prophetic words... most of them nameless and faceless. God would not speak to that many people if he were not up to something. My six year old grandson told his mom, "*President Trump Changed the World.*"

In the life and ministry of Jesus, we see a Prophetic thread, from Genesis through the New Testament. It is confirmed in the first chapter of Matthew that documents Jesus' lineage. God protected His word throughout the generations. God gives us the Prophetic word so when things look impossible, we can remain firm in our convictions. 2 Peter 1:19 (NIV) says,

A BOTCHED ELECTION

We also have the Prophetic message as something completely reliable, and you will do well to pay attention to it, as to a light shining in a dark place, until the day dawns and the morning star rises in your hearts.

There are always signs in the natural that confirm the movement of God. The Red Sea parting, the walls of Jericho coming down, the Eastern star confirming Jesus' birth. When God speaks a word everything in the natural and spiritual has to come in agreement with His divine declaration. When something moves in the Heavenlies there is a demonstrative response in the Earth realm.

A BOTCHED ELECTION

There is language throughout the Bible that verifies this. Psalms 29:11 (NIV) says, *"The voice of the Lord makes the deer give birth, And strips the forests bare; And in His temple, everyone says, "Glory!"* Some Earthquakes happened in very key Biblical areas that coincided with critical dates in our nation (November 3 and January 6). We can say coincidental, perhaps.

Moreover, December 1620 was the birth of this nation; we are literally at the 400-year mark. 400 years is significant in the Bible; it is the cleansing of a nation. God left the children of Israel in Egyptian bondage until the iniquity of the Amorites had been fulfilled. Genesis 5:16 says, *"But in the fourth generation they shall return here, for the iniquity of the Amorites is not yet complete.*" The cup of iniquity is full in this nation and God is now obligated, by His character and nature to respond.

For every true Prophetic word, there will always be Satanic opposition, but God will strengthen the Prophets to endure the contradiction. When God sent Elijah to King Ahab (1 Kings 18:1) Jezebel arose to counteract and neuter God's assignment through Elijah. He also releases faith to believe and endure.

Anna, the Prophet, remained in the temple worshipping, fasting, and praying until Jesus appeared (Luke 2:37). Did people think Anna was crazy? Of course, they did. A Prophetic word arrests you. Ezekiel was picked up by the word of prophecy and hung in the balance between Heaven and Earth (Ezekiel 8:3). Your life gets put on hold for a while and you have to resist the temptation to want to get back to normal.

In my experience, the closer an event gets to manifestation the heavier the burden gets and the more intense the warfare becomes. Paul said, "*There were many devils at the open door that God had prepared for him,(1 Corinthians 16:8)*." It is also important to remember God operates from the Kingdom which has an entirely different set of laws. We say what God has given us to say and we cannot control His methods, His timing, or His actions.

A BOTCHED ELECTION

God is draining the swamps in the government and the church. It is happening and the warfare is harder than anticipated. Prophets are jumping ship because it is so uncomfortable, and they want to get back to their agenda and abandon God's. I believe the real objective has nothing to do with the Presidential Election but what is in the swamp.

A BOTCHED ELECTION

An American Patriot

One of the most fascinating experiences for me was I watched the Constitution of the United States come alive. I used to believe it was not written for me because of Slavery. It may not have initially been written with me in mind, but I can now claim it as my own. The intricacies and brilliance of this document can be used to bring a quality of life that I have never experienced. The Radical

A BOTCHED ELECTION

Left desires to do away with the Constitution and weaponize it against the American People so they could make up their own rules and laws.

But those that were fighting this election battle by the books, it became their greatest ally. Some State Officials did not even know their constitutional rights. It gives us power unlike any other nation and that is what makes us stand apart. We see it in motion every day. The wisdom in which this document was crafted can only be from the Holy Spirit. One atrocity is their efforts to impeach President Trump. Below is the definition of Impeachment according to the Constitution.

Judgment in Cases of Impeachment shall not extend further than to removal from Office, and disqualification to hold and enjoy any Office of honor, Trust or Profit under the United States: but the Party convicted shall nevertheless be liable and subject to Indictment, Trial, Judgment, and Punishment, according to Law.

According to the Legal Information Institute's Constitutional clarification:

The impeachment provisions of the Constitution were derived from English practice, but there are important differences. In England, impeachment had a far broader scope. While impeachment was a device to remove from office one who abused his office or misbehaved but who was protected by the Crown, it could be used against anyone—office holder or not—and was penal in nature, with possible penalties of fines, imprisonment, or even death. By contrast, the American impeachment process is remedial, not penal: it is limited to office holders, and judgments are limited to no more than removal from office and disqualification to hold future office.

In essence, you cannot impeach a person who is NOT currently holding an office. Therefore, I am questioning why they are trying to impeach someone who is not the legal President? Unless he is the legal

President? When President Nixon was impeached because of the Watergate Scandal, the moment he resigned the Impeachment Process stopped.

On the Horizon

Revival is imminent, we will not be able to escape it. How it will affect your life depends on what side of the fence you are on. The reverential fear of God is going to consume the globe, unlike anything we have ever seen. If you are playing church, are on the fence, operating in witchcraft, harboring bitterness, manipulating God's people, in any form, or are lukewarm it is time to get it right, especially Prophetic leaders.

A BOTCHED ELECTION

Ananias and Sapphira lied to the Holy Spirit and the FEAR of the LORD struck the hearts of all those who HEARD (Acts 5:5). I remember going to a revival meeting in the early '90s where the power of God consumed the building and people were laying slain under the power of the Holy Ghost on the sidewalk. People were walking out of the building fully intoxicated and staggering under the power. Once again, it is happening.

We are in a period of deep self-inspection. Instead of worrying if the Prophets missed it what condition is your heart in? Examine yourself and see if you are in the faith? Search every nook and cranny of your soul and see if there is any wicked or twisted way in you. Repent and bear fruit that supports an inward change. Rend your hearts and not your garments. Let the PRIEST that minister to the Lord weeps BETWEEN THE PORCH AND THE ALTAR, (Joel 2:17). Whatever you fail to kill will ultimately kill you. The Lord's rebuke and correction of me during an early morning visitation:

"To the angel of the church in Ephesus write:

These are the words of him who holds the seven stars in his right hand and walks among the seven golden lampstands. I know your deeds, your hard work, and your perseverance. I know that you cannot tolerate wicked people, that you have tested those who claim to be apostles but are not and have found them false. You have persevered and have endured hardships for my name and have not grown weary. Yet I hold this against you: You have forsaken the love you had at first. Consider how far you have fallen! Repent and do the things you did at first. If you do not repent, I will come to you and remove your lampstand from its place (Revelations 2:1-5, NIV).

My heart shattered into a million pieces, and I just began to weep and repent. It is easy to wield the knife at others but difficult to turn the knife on yourself."

We are going to see one of the largest class-action lawsuits and

A BOTCHED ELECTION

Antitrust cases in American History against Big Tech. I was alerted of this in the spirit, a few weeks ago, when I received an email from Instagram that said, *"By using this platform I agree to not being involved in a class-action lawsuit against them."*

I had a dream several years ago about the Federal Reserve building in Atlanta. The building was incredibly old, in a remote place, and looked abandoned. But on the building written in bold black letters was WOMEN'S CONCOURSE. A concourse is where pathways meet, i.e., airports, train stations, hotels. There are very few women millionaires unless they inherited it or married into it. We will see more, stand-alone, women millionaires in American History. There is going to be a demonstrative wave of supernatural wealth transfer.

The Next Ten Years

God is stirring again the winds of revival. The healing wells are trembling and shaking. COVID19 was Satan's attempt to clog up the wells. Genesis 26:18 (NIV) says,

> *Isaac dug again the wells of water which had been dug in the days of his father Abraham, for the Philistines had stopped them up after the death of Abraham."*

A BOTCHED ELECTION

Many will be miraculously healed; sickness and disease will fall off like meat on a bone. Your years of trauma are over. Affliction will not rise a second time (Nahum 1:9). God will restore all that you lost in this last season (Joel 2:25). Do not fret or worry because GOD is faithful. He has raised an end-time Prophetic army that will not be rivaled. If you have been praying and contending for the faith (Jude 1:5), this is the hour you have been anticipating. We will see a move of the Holy Spirit unlike anything we have ever experienced.

Prophets who live in the Heartland (OKC, CO, NE, NM, TX) your days of dryness are over; a fresh wind is blowing your way. The lingering effects of the dust bowl have ended. Springs will rise in the dry places.

Prophetic companies are forming as we speak. God has ordained many Prophets that have been waiting on man's approval. I hear the LORD say, "Approved!" You are now being DEPLOYED. This is not a call to anarchy or rebellion but obedience to His agenda and His word.

The fear of the Lord will sweep this nation like a Tsunami and your Earthly ministries will crumble if they are not built on the rock. In the next few months, COVID19 will leave as swiftly as it came. In 2021 we will still feel the shaking from 2020 but then we will experience a decade of great peace, financial stability, and safety.

A BOTCHED ELECTION

TO THE FAITHFUL, I hear the Lord say Prepare, Prepare, Prepare. This is a season of separation from people that are not part of God's plan for you or do not have the stamina to travel the rugged terrain. They are not bad people they are just not good for you.

Do not weep or delay...let go. Honor the time you had together and gird up your Prophetic garment and move. Kingdom connections are coming. People that have been written off, mocked, overlooked, and abused in churches will now become the Apple of God's eye. All eyes are watching; Global and domestic. Swift judgment will come on those who have mocked God:

A BOTCHED ELECTION

God will bring in the prodigals; those who have resisted the false religious structures that fleshly men have tried to mandate. The church will be judged swiftly, and many doors will close never to reopen. The yoke of the enemy will be broken off of every wayward and rebellious child. Especially those that were raised in the church.

This is the hour of the prodigal. They are coming home restored and repented. The bondage of the enemy is being destroyed. Prophets of God position yourself for a fresh wave of His anointing, a spiritual upgrade, and release of supernatural revelation to understand His word. This will be the hour of the PURE Prophet, Prophets not for Profit. It shall be as the Lord has said.

Church leaders beware! You do not own people, God does. They are not your servants or minions. Your responsibility has been to help them grow in God and know that they are loved by Him. The hour of the fleshly, selfish, greedy church is over!

Angelic activity will significantly increase, and many will be made aware (2 Kings 19:35, Psalms 103:20). We are entering a season of great Mercy. The mercy of God is being made available to all those who have been crying out. God has heard your cry (Hebrews 4:16).

Without ever going into a church, thousands will repent

because God will meet them where they are. Kingdom businesses will flourish over the next four years, unlike anything you have ever seen. We are entering the end-time transfer of wealth and God is snatching money out of the hands of the wicked and putting it into the hands of the righteous (Proverbs 13:22).

The marketplace is rumbling, and God's hand is on Kingdom entrepreneurs (Ecclesiastes 9:10). God is breathing on the true church as He did in the days of Elijah. The dry bones will live again (Ezekiel 37:1-14). Stand firm, guard your heart, trust God, and receive the joy of the Lord.

The End Time Harvest

It amazes me how people who say they love God do not believe they should vote in agreement with their faith. Do you have God's heart? or do you love His hand? The main reason God chose President Trump was that he was a businessman with an anointing for business, not a Politician. He is, in my knowledge, the only President that did not take a salary. The stock market flourished under his first term and when Twitter and Facebook banned him they lost 51 billion from their stock portfolio in a matter of days. He wants to move back to "Made in the USA," We will no longer have to contend with foreign influence. Pastor Dana Coverstone said, "*He saw in a dream money being snatched out of Washington. Ripped out of the hands of the wicked and put into the hands of the just.*" This end-time transfer of wealth is to fund Kingdom Agendas.

As the Body of Christ takes on a new shape and form and as our nation is reborn, we have to be willing to have difficult conversations. We must be willing to surrender ourselves in prayer and get the mind of God. The Prophetic ministry is going to be moved front and center.

A BOTCHED ELECTION

It will be an integral part of the end-time army so prepared we must be. This has been a Bootcamp experience for me. Sharpening my sword and making my vision laser focus. For those that are prepared, we will soar like Eagles into dimensions of ministry that we have never experienced. We are moving back into the tent revivals and healing crusades because God needs an army that is ready and positioned to engage in the battle of the ages.

I, without a doubt, know that greater days are ahead for the church. I also know that we are closer to the coming of the Lord than ever before. All hands must be on deck and our robes must be drenched in the blood of the lamb for the final curtain call. I believe we are in the

A BOTCHED ELECTION

most exciting times the church has ever seen. Jesus said, *"Look, I am coming soon! My reward is with me, and I will give to each person according to what they have done* (Revelations 22:12, NIV).

Michael Lindell's documentary Absolute Proof is the full story and length the enemy and the Radical Left did in an effort to fix this election. God executes judgement on the wicked and we will prevail.

Finally, I want to say thank you for trusting that I had something worthwhile to say. I have presented this information in the most comprehensive way I knew how but would love to hear your thoughts

VISIT MY WEBSITE
WWW.YVONNECAMPER.ORG

[i] "Kim Clement: Last Prophetic Word Over America." Youtube, Uploaded by Joe Joe Dawson, 22 Sep. 2020
https://www.youtube.com/watch?v=a5v9SCLgAGI

[ii] "The Coming Shift, Are You Really A Christian." Youtube, Uploaded by Yvonne D. Camper, 12 Apr 2018,
https://www.youtube.com/watch?v=oVkrkEaBaqE&t=58s

[iii] The President Trump Prophecy. Directed by Stephan Schultze Reel Works Studio, 2018. YouTube, uploaded by New Video Group, 4 Mar 2019,
https://www.youtube.com/watch?v=EWtTrTGCI-A

[iv] The President Trump Card. Directed by Dinesh D'Souza, Bruce Schooley, Debbie D'Souza, 2020. YouTube uploaded by Quiver. 20 Oct 2020,
https://www.youtube.com/watch?v=FPCFrA-Qv0E

[v] "Steven Springer: Valkyrie Will Fall and Will Not Sing." YouTube, uploaded by King of Kings Worship Center, 8 Jan. 2021,
https://www.youtube.com/watch?v=CVY_UJVo5Wo

[vi] "Former Facebook Insider Calls for Shutting Down Conservative Influencers." Rumbo, uploaded by Bongino Report, 17 Jan. 2021, https://rumble.com/vcxqav-former-facebook-insider-calls-for-shutting-down-conservative-influencers.htmlchur

[vii] "Church in America, Wake Up! | Jeremiah 6:16-19 | Gary Hamrick." Youtube, Uploaded by Cornerstone Chapel – Leesburg, 18, Oct 2020, https://www.youtube.com/watch?v=10HRwSKTUiU

[viii] "Draining of the Prophetic Swamps." Youtube, uploaded by Yvonne D. Camper, 13 Nov 2020. https://www.youtube.com/watch?v=MK2x0xc4Xv8

[ix] "7 Days of Dominion Day 6 - Prophetic Word - Corona Virus and the rise of the church." Youtube, uploaded by Yvonne D. Camper 18, Mar 2020. https://www.youtube.com/watch?v=HYnE-0uSxlY&t=1198s

[x] Owens, Caitlin. "The swing states where the pandemic is raging." Axios, 25 Oct 2020, https://www.axios.com/coronavirus-2020-election-senate-59e4f2bb-93e2-4ebb-84ad-4fe3aed6e043.html

[xi] Queally, James. "Hawthorne men accused in voter fraud plot to obtain 8,000 mail ballots for 'nonexistent or deceased' persons." Los Angeles Times, 17, Nov. 2020.

[xii] Kyle Olson, Michigan State Rep. Cynthia Johnson: Biden 'owes' Detroit.' BreitBart, 11 Dec. 2020

[xiii] Amanda Prestigiacomo. "WATCH: Democrat Rep. Cynthia Johnson Threatens President Trump Supporters: 'Make Them Pay'
"This is just a warning to you President Trumpers: Be careful, walk lightly, we ain't playing with you." Daily Wire 09, Dec. 2020

[xiv] Watch Democrat Rep. LOSE HER MIND During MI Fraud Hearing (True Insanity Unfolds)." Youtube, Uploaded by Admiral Addy, 3 Dec 2020.
https://www.youtube.com/watch?v=mhP_d17fMrQ

[xv] "Joe Biden Crime Bill Speech in Senate - November 18 1993 - Full speech." Uploaded by High Horse, 01, Jun 2020.
https://www.youtube.com/watch?v=zCaO0NvadlQ

[xvi] Suzanne Downing. "How could the 'bellwether counties' get it so wrong?. 6 Nov 2020. Must Read Alaska. How could the 'bellwether counties' get it so wrong? https://mustreadalaska.com/how-could-the-bellwether-counties-get-it-so-wrong/

[xvii] "How social media company Parler may be able to compete with Twitter." Youtube, Uploaded by CNBC Television, 12 Nov 2020.
https://www.youtube.com/watch?v=oL078Bq0PyU

[xviii] San Francisco CBSlocal.com. "VP Residence Renovation Mystery: 2 Months Into Office, Kamala Harris Is Still Waiting for Home." 27 MAR 2021. https://sanfrancisco.cbslocal.com/2021/03/27/vice-president-kamala-harris-living-suitcases/

www.ingramcontent.com/pod-product-compliance
Lightning Source LLC
LaVergne TN
LVHW051121080426
835510LV00018B/2160